Leader's Guide for group study of

BE COMMITTED

Warren Wiersbe

Leader's Guide prepared by
MIKE FRANS

Six Reproducible Response Sheets are included in a removable center section.

A DIVISION OF SCRIPTURE PRESS PUBLICATIONS INC.
USA CANADA ENGLAND

Scriptures are taken from the *Holy Bible, New International Version,* © 1973, 1978, 1984, International Bible Society. Used by permission of Zondervan Bible Publishers.

1 2 3 4 5 6 7 8 9 10 Printing/Year 97 96 95 94 93

ISBN: 1-56476-068-5
©1993 by Victor Books/SP Publications, Inc. All rights reserved.
Printed in the United States of America.

VICTOR BOOKS
A division of SP Publications, Inc.
1825 College Avenue, Wheaton, Illinois, 60187

THE PLACE TO BEGIN

Before you start flipping through this Leader's Guide, stop for a couple of minutes and read pages 4–7. These pages will:
- Tell you what you'll need to know to prepare each lesson.
- Introduce different methods of leading group interaction.
- Help you evaluate how you're doing as a group leader.

KNOW YOUR GROUP

Picture the individuals who make up your group. What do you know about them? What do you need to know to lead them effectively? Here are a few suggestions:
- Develop warm relationships—get to know group members by name. Find ways to help members get to know each other as well.
- Find out what your group members already know and what they would like to know.
- Be a good listener.
- Promote an attitude of acceptance and respect among group members.

GET READY TO LEAD

If you are a little unsure of yourself because you're leading a group of adults for the first time, then follow the LESSON PLAN outlines for each session.

Using the guided discovery learning approach, each chapter will contain at least three sections:

- *Launching the Lesson*—activities that begin focusing on group members' needs.
- *Discovering God's Principles*—creative ways to communicate Bible truth.
- *Applying the Truth*—application activities that relate Bible truth to everyday life.

Some sessions may contain additional, optional sections such as:
- *Building the Body*—icebreakers and activities to help group members build relationships.
- *Prayer Time*—suggestions for praying together as a group.

REMEMBER THE BASICS

Read the entire text and this Leader's Guide. Underline important passages in the text and make notes as ideas come to you. Note any activities in the guide that take advance planning or preparation.

Follow these steps in planning each session:
- Make a brief outline of your lesson plan.
- Formulate and *write down* all the discussion questions you intend to use.
- Note all activities and interaction methods you plan to implement.
- Gather all the materials you will need for the session.

Each session should focus on at least one, and often several, Bible truths that can be applied directly to the lives of your group members. Encourage group members to bring their Bibles to each session and use them. It's also a good idea to have several modern-speech translations on hand for the purpose of comparison.

USE A VARIETY OF INTERACTION METHODS

Response Sheets

Several Response Sheets are provided for you in the removable center section of this guide. Response Sheets are designed to extend the lesson's impact.

The Response Sheets in this guide will help you enliven your sessions and encourage group involvement. They are numbered consecutively (Response Sheet 1 – Response Sheet 6) and show with what sessions they should be used. The guide gives specific directions for when and how to use each Response Sheet in the lesson material.

Brainstorming

Announce the question or topic to be "stormed." Group members may make as many spontaneous suggestions as possible, not waiting to be called on. Don't allow anyone to criticize the suggestions. List suggestions on a chalkboard or poster board; when all are in, have the class evaluate the ideas. This method loosens up the group, involves nonparticipants, and produces new insights.

Group Bible Study

Each person should have her or his Bible open. Ask questions that will help the group learn what the passage you are studying says. Encourage sharing of insights as the group discusses the interpretations of the passage and its application to current needs. Always summarize findings. This method makes group members think; it shows them how to study the Bible on their own and it increases participation and involvement.

Discovery Groups
Divide the group into small groups of three to six persons. Appoint a leader for each group or let groups select their own leaders. Assign a topic to each group. Several—or all—groups may discuss the same topic if necessary. Allow 5–8 minutes for discussion in the groups, then reconvene and get reports from group leaders. Jot findings on a chalkboard or poster board for discussion. Since many persons are freer to express themselves in small groups, this method provides maximum participation opportunity.

Role Play
Two or more group members, without advance notice or written scripts, act out a situation or relationship. Give them directions as to the kind of people they are to represent and the situation in which they find themselves. They speak extemporaneously. This method helps people "feel" situations, gives them opportunity to try different solutions, and creates interest in the lesson.

Skit
Have members read the parts of a brief script that highlights a point, provokes discussion, or presents information. Skits provide sessions with stimulating variety.

Diads
Like *Discovery Groups*, except that there are only two people, sitting next to each other, in each "group." (If a person is left out in the pairing off, assign him to one of the twosomes.) This method makes it easy for shy persons to participate.

Discussion
In discussion, members interact not only with the group leader but with one another. Usually discussion is started by the group leader's asking a question to which there is more than a single acceptable answer. A member will respond to a question, someone else may disagree with him, and a third person may have additional comments. The leader is responsible for starting the discussion, keeping it "on track" by asking leading questions as necessary, and summarizing it after contributions cease. If a discussion gets out of hand and rambles, much of its value is lost.

Here are a few guidelines for leading discussion:
- Maintain a relaxed, informal atmosphere.

- Don't call on people by name to take part unless you are sure they are willing to do so.
- Give a person lots of time to answer a question. If necessary, restate the question casually and informally.
- Acknowledge any contribution, regardless of its merit.
- Don't correct or embarrass a person who gives a wrong answer. Thank him or her; then ask, "What do the rest of you think?"
- If someone monopolizes the discussion, say, "On the next question, let's hear from someone who hasn't spoken yet."
- If someone goes off on a tangent, wait for him or her to draw a breath, then say, "Thanks for those interesting comments. Now let's get back to . . ." and mention the subject under consideration, or ask or restate a question that will bring the discussion back on target.
- If someone asks a question, allow others in the group to give their answers before you give yours.

EVALUATE YOUR EFFECTIVENESS

After each session, ask yourself the following questions:

_____ How well did each group member understand the lesson goals?

_____ How many group members actually took part in the lesson?

_____ Could I use other interaction methods to increase group member interest and participation?

_____ Did I nurture personal relationships with my group members?

_____ How well did I prepare the lesson?

_____ How did group members react to me as a group leader?

_____ What do I need to do to become a better group leader?

Session One

YOU CAN'T RUN AWAY

TEXT, CHAPTER 1

Session Topic
Trusting God for our future begins by trusting Him with our past.

Session Goals
1. To identify reasons why people may run from their past.
2. To examine the results of those who run from their past.
3. To explore the resources available for starting over with God.

Materials Needed
√ Bible
√ *Be Committed*
√ Copies of Response Sheet 1 for small groups
√ Pencils

Special Preparation
1. Try to distribute the texts to members prior to the first meeting and ask them to read chapter 1.
2. Read through the Book of Ruth to get a feel for the main characters. Look for evidence of her commitment to the Lord and His people. Also, use a Bible handbook or Henrietta Mears' book, *What the Bible Is All About,* to get a general background of the book and its themes. Note any points you want to emphasize.

LESSON PLAN

Building the Body *(15 minutes)*

Ask members to recall examples from our culture that commitment is no longer an esteemed value. For instance, the climbing divorce rate, little loyalty to churches, labor unions, political parties and other organizations, a declining consumer loyalty to products, having fewer close friends than in the past. Ask them to divide into smaller groups and answer the following: What evidences of lack of commitment have you observed, and how have you been affected by it?

Launching the Lesson *(5–10 minutes)*

Say: **Commitment as a value was at an all-time low during the days of the Judges, but Ruth went against the trend. Her extended family model was that of running from past failures. What reasons or circumstances might cause any of us to run from our problems?** After members have responded, mention some of the reasons Elimelech and Naomi may have run from their past. Point out such reasons as tough times, refusal to wait on God's provisions, bad advice, unbelief, and disobedience. Then say: **Choices have consequences, whether physical, emotional, or spiritual. To avoid such traps, we will analyze both negative and positive alternatives in handling our past failures.**

Discovering God's Principles *(35–40 minutes)*

Discuss: **In Ruth 1:1-5, what were some of the consequences of Elimelech's decision? What made his decision so wrong?** Refer to the Wiersbe text for ideas, if needed.

Divide members into five groups, appoint a leader in each group, and give him or her copies of Response Sheet 1 and pencils to distribute. After giving members a brief overview of the grief process that Naomi most likely encountered, assign one aspect of the grief process to each group. Ask them to examine together and record their observations about Naomi's handling of grief and to do the group exercise on Response Sheet 1. If time permits, encourage them to compare Naomi's experience with Job's.

After about 15–20 minutes, reassemble the groups and ask leaders to share their group's analysis and advice, beginning with the

"denial" stage. Explore the following questions: (Be sure to participate yourself.)
- *How normal is it that Naomi responded to her painful past in blaming God? (Ruth 1:19-20) What similar circumstances have you experienced? How did you respond to God?*
- *How would you contrast the starting over process by each of the three widows? (Ruth 1:15-18) What experiences have you had in starting over? What wisdom with hindsight would you now share with someone like Naomi or Ruth who was starting over?*

Applying the Truth (5 minutes)

Read Ruth's pledge of commitment before Naomi and the Lord in Ruth 1:16-17. Ask members to pair up and pray conversationally their own pledge of commitment to follow Christ as their Lord and Savior wherever He may lead and in whatever circumstances they may face. Remind members that trusting God with our future also means trusting Him with our past and present.

Before members leave, present them with the following recommended books for starting over:

Where Is God When It Hurts? by Philip Yancey.
Rebuilding Your Broken World, by Gordon MacDonald.
Forgive and Forget: Healing the Hurts We Don't Deserve, by Lewis Smedes.

Also suggest that some members may need professional Christian guidance in starting over, or may need a specialized support group.

ASSIGNMENT

1. Ask each person to do a brief time line of his or her life, showing dates, places or people that God used at turning points. Ask that they compare notes on their time lines as they read chapter 2 of the text about Ruth's turning points.
2. Ask one or two members to volunteer to share a book review based on one listed in *Applying the Truth* during the fourth session.
3. Urge one or two members to volunteer to share at the next meeting the time lines of their turning points and God's providence in their lives.

Session Two

THE GREATEST OF THESE

TEXT, CHAPTER 2

Session Topic
God's grace motivates us to live a life filled with faith, hope, and love.

Session Goals
1. To recognize God's providence in the turning points of our lives.
2. To analyze the change process in our lives as a result of faith, hope, and love.
3. To make a biblical case for becoming a difference maker in the lives of others.

Materials Needed
√ Bible
√ *Be Committed*
√ Poster board and markers for each member

Special Preparation
1. Call the volunteers who agreed to share their time line of the turning points and evidence of God's providence in their lives.
2. If possible, locate a copy of Howard Vos' book, *Effective Bible Study,* and read the 15 questions to ask when doing a character study. See the chapter titled, "The Biographical Method." Apply these questions as you continue to work through the Books of Ruth and Esther.
3. Reproduce Visual Sketch 1 using poster board and markers.

LESSON PLAN

Building the Body *(5 minutes)*

Ask members to divide into smaller groups to share the answer to the question: **If your life could be made into a movie, novel, or song, what would its title be, and why?** Suggest that each person borrow a classical or current title from a movie, book, or song that might creatively suggest the theme for his or her life story.

Launching the Lesson *(20 minutes)*

Introduce the volunteers who will share the time line of the turning points in their lives for about two or three minutes each. Thank them for their willingness to share.

Then distribute a poster board and marker to each member. Ask them to creatively outline the turning points of their lives, possibly using footprints, a table of contents for a book, titles for the acts or scenes of a play. Encourage them to use simple words or phrases for each turning point, such as a date in time, a place, influential persons, or events, that could give the big picture of their lives at a glance. Instruct them to be prepared to share their stories in a two-minute time frame using their visual aids.

When all are finished, ask them to pair up and share their life stories with each other. After members have shared their stories, ask them to go back to their visual aids and interact with their partners about when Christ became real to them. Have them put a cross on their visual aids to show that turning point.

Ask them to discuss together: **What differences in your life did you notice after you developed a relationship with Christ compared with before He became real to you? What evidence do you see of His grace at work in your life even before you met Christ?**

Suggest, for instance, that God may have allowed certain circumstances or brought certain people into their lives, as a part of His providence.

Point out that in today's session we will be focusing on the changes in Ruth and Naomi and on God's providence in their lives.

Discovering God's Principles *(30–40 minutes)*

Say to the group: **God is able to move us from a life of bitterness to one of blessedness. What changes are evident in Naomi's life** from Ruth 2:1 to Ruth 2:19-20? How do you account for such changes?

A FAITH THAT WORKS!	
FAITH (Trust) (What <u>God</u> must do)	WORKS (Action) (What <u>I</u> must do)
1. 2. 3.	1. 2. 3.

Visual Sketch 1
Identifying God's part will help us have a faith that works.

As you move on to address the change in circumstances in Ruth's life (Ruth 2), display the poster of Visual Sketch 1. Say: **The explanation for the changes in Ruth's circumstances is rooted in certain conditions, such as living by faith in the Lord, by His grace, and in His hope. In order to have a faith that works, we must identify our part and God's part. As we look at the life of Ruth in chapters 1 and 2, let's see if we can list areas she would have to trust to God (things only He could do) and list areas where she would need her own plan of action.** Remind them of James 2:20, that "faith without works is dead." Instruct them to use their texts and/or their Bibles to supply examples.

After recording their responses, come back to God's part. Ask members to refer to the five parallels in chapter 2 of the Wiersbe text in the second main section, where Boaz is compared to Christ. Ask: **What additional areas of trust could be added to the column marked "Faith" (what God must do)?**

Point out to members that to live by faith is not without its obstacles. Ask: **What obstacles to faith did Ruth have to overcome?** (Possible responses could include: being a woman, being a widow, being poor, being an alien.) Ask members to divide into groups of three or four and ask them to share one or more obstacles they have faced and possibly overcome as they tried to live by faith. Encourage them to use a specific time or event when this occurred.

Applying the Truth   *(10 minutes)*

Say: **Just as Ruth became a difference-maker and change-agent in Naomi's life, we too can become difference-makers in the** lives of others. Let's close by looking at those who made a difference in the lives of others.

Instruct members to divide into three groups to look briefly at how the following may have made an eternal difference in another's life:

Group #1 The difference Stephen may have made in Paul's life (Acts 7:54–8:3);

Group #2 The difference Ananias may have made in Paul's life (Acts 9:10-19);

Group #3 The difference Barnabas may have made in Paul's life (Acts 9:20-30).

Challenge people in the group to recall someone God used in their lives to make a life-changing difference, a Boaz-type person. Ask them to pray in pairs thanking God for that one who made such a difference.

Then ask them to pray that God will use them to make a difference in a Ruth-type person—someone in need of and likely receptive to the grace of God.

ASSIGNMENT

1. Ask members to read chapter 3 of the text, looking for the steps to a deeper walk with God. Have them ask: **What need do I presently sense for a deeper walk with the Lord?**
2. Urge them to write and mail a letter of gratitude to someone God has used in their lives to make an eternal difference.

Looking Ahead

Urge three or four of your members to form a tour group to take a tour through your church on a Sunday morning. They should start with the parking lot and move to all the places a guest might stop during his or her stay. Let the group know that their goal is to develop a seeker-sensitive approach to the church and to note questions or obstacles a newcomer may face. Encourage them to take notes and be prepared to share their observations in a few weeks. Perhaps they could pretend that Ruth the Moabitess will be attending your church. What questions might she have? What feelings? How would you make her feel welcome?

Also, a separate group could agree to visit a totally different church, perhaps a cross-cultural one, and could record their observations and feelings as outsiders.

Session Three

THE MIDNIGHT MEETING

TEXT, CHAPTER 3

Session Topic
To enter a deeper relationship with Christ, we must meet God's conditions.

Session Goals
1. To examine our desire for a deeper relationship with Christ.
2. To identify ways to maintain a relationship with Christ.
3. To convince members that God's commitment to them will enable them to carry out their commitment to God.

Materials Needed
√ Bible
√ *Be Committed*
√ Hymn books with the hymn, "How Firm a Foundation"
√ Note cards, pencils
√ Visual Sketch 2, pencils

Special Preparation
1. Read Colossians 3:1-17 noting the things we should "put off" and "put on" as believers in Christ.
2. Copies of an enlarged Visual Sketch 2 for each member.

LESSON PLAN

Building the Body (5 minutes)

Say: **Life's big events require major preparations and conditions. Weddings, house and car purchases, moves all make certain demands on us. What preparations and conditions have you had to carry out for major events?**

Afterward, say: Just as one must prepare for a major commitment like marriage or buying a home, so must we prepare to enter a relationship with Christ.

Launching the Lesson (15 minutes)

Distribute note cards and pencils. Ask each member to take the following self-assessment of needs and desires to deepen his or her relationship with Christ. Instruct people to make four line graphs, each one scaled from zero to ten, on each side of the card. At the top of side one, put "My Desires," and on side two, "My Actual Involvement." Read the four following categories and as you do, ask them to put a key word by each scale and their self-assessment. Zero means no desire, and ten, great desire. On side two, zero means no involvement, and ten, consistent involvement.

#1	**God's Word**	How would I assess my listening relationship to God?
#2	**Prayer**	How would I assess my talking relationship with God?
#3	**Fellowship**	How would I assess my relationships with God's people?
#4	**Service**	How would I assess my involvement in meaningful ministry and outreach?

After the self-assessment, ask group members to discuss in pairs: **How does my desire level compare to my involvement level? What changes (upward or downward) have I noticed in the past six months? What explanations may account for such changes? What barriers do I see to moving my actual involvement closer to my desire to deepen my walk with Christ?**

Discovering God's Principles (20–25 minutes)

State that the starting place for entering a deeper relationship with God is repentance—a change of mind that leads to a change of behavior. Ask members to read Psalm 51 silently as you read it aloud. Urge them to make this their prayer for renewal.

Then ask a volunteer to read Proverbs 28:13. Discuss together: **What needs to be coupled with David's prayer of confession? What aspects of repentance and forgiveness are God's part, and what are our own responsibilities?**

SPRING CLEANING!	
(Colossians 3:1-14)	
TAKING OFF THE "GRAVE CLOTHES"	PUTTING ON THE "GRACE CLOTHES"
1.	1.
2.	2.
3.	3.
4.	4.
5.	5.
6.	6.
7.	7.

Visual Sketch 2
In the Christian life, clothes make the Christian; we must choose our wardrobe.

Remind members of the fivefold preparation Ruth made in order to present herself to Boaz, a process comparable to our having a deeper relationship with Christ. Distribute copies of Visual Sketch 2 along with pencils. Say: **Let's focus on Ruth's third step of preparation, her changing of clothes to get ready for a wedding (Ruth 3:3). In the Christian walk, clothes make the Christian, and we have the responsibility of doing spring cleaning with our "closets" and choosing a new wardrobe.** Ask them to divide into small groups, quickly reading through Colossians 3:1-17. They should list the "graveclothes" of the old life that need to be removed, and list the "grace clothes" of the new life that need to be put on.

Discuss: **If we are Christians, why do you think we still need to "put to death" aspects of our old way of life? Also, if we have the Holy Spirit indwelling, why must we continue to put on the new self? What does this tell us about God's part versus our part in our spiritual renewal?**

Now ask members to look over the old and new "wardrobes." Instruct them to look at the two lists on their Visual Sketch 2 sheets and put a mental asterisk next to one of the old pieces of clothing that they must rid themselves of, and a mental asterisk by one of the new pieces of clothing that might possibly replace the old garment. Then ask group members to pray silently for the person on their left in their small group about getting rid of the old clothes they have noted before the Lord. Next ask them to pray for the person on their right about the new clothes they have determined before the Lord that they would like to put on. Have them close by praying for themselves silently, making a renewed commitment to the Lord to clean house and have a new wardrobe. Read Ruth's words of commitment before the group reassembles: "All that you say to me I will do" (Ruth 3:5).

Applying the Truth *(10 minutes)*

Say: **One of the barriers to deepening our relationship to Christ is fear—fear of failure, fear of our past track record, fear of being inadequate. We are often afraid that it all depends on our efforts, our commitment. But we must continue to develop our listening relationship with the Lord, listening to His Word rather than to our feelings.** Read 2 Timothy 2:11-13. Ask: **Who has the greatest responsibility and who takes the greatest risks in maintaining our relationship with Christ, us or Him?**

Then ask members to turn to page 47 of their text and look for the paragraph that begins, "Fear not." Ask each member to look up one of the references and to read his or her verse about God's assurance to His servants from the past. Ask: **What bases of assurance seem to come through again and again?** (The presence and power of the Lord)

Ask members to recite after you the words from Hebrews 13:6. Then distribute copies of the hymnal and invite members to sing the hymn, "How Firm a Foundation," encouraging them to think of singing to one another these words of encouragement.

ASSIGNMENT

1. Ask members to read chapter 4 of the text, looking for all the changes in Ruth's life since she met Boaz. Ask them to list changes that have occurred in their lives since meeting Christ.
2. Invite members to read through the interlude to the Book of Ruth in the text and underline one or two practical lessons from the Book of Ruth that have encouraged them. They should prepare to share their reflections at the next meeting.
3. Prepare members by letting them know in advance that at the close of the next session, we will celebrate our commitment to Christ in a candlelight Communion service.

Session Four

LOVE FINDS A WAY

TEXT, CHAPTER 4

Session Topic
We can leave behind a legacy that will impact our world for Christ.

Session Goals
1. To chart the spiritual impact of our own family tree.
2. To develop inductive skills in assessing the life and legacy of Bible characters.
3. To count the costs of our commitment to Christ and to celebrate His commitment to us.

Materials Needed
√ Bible
√ *Be Committed*
√ Copies of Response Sheet 2, pencils
√ Blank sheets of paper for each member
√ Hymn books or chorus sheets for each member

Special Preparation
1. Reproduce Visual Sketch 3 using poster board and markers.
2. Call and remind the volunteer(s) from Session One to be prepared to do their book review this session.
3. If your church permits celebration of Communion by lay people, obtain elements for a brief Communion service to be conducted during the application section. (Option: Use candlelight for atmosphere. Invite a leader from your church or the group to assist you in conducting the Communion celebration.
4. Look up the words "Redeemer" and "Redemption" in a Bible dictionary.

LESSON PLAN

Building the Body *(5–8 minutes)*

Introduce the member(s) who volunteered to share a book review in Session One.

As an alternative (if no volunteers exist), follow up on last session's assignment and ask members to share what they highlighted as they read Wiersbe's "Interlude" reflections on pages 67–70.

Launching the Lesson *(10 minutes)*

Distribute blank sheets of paper and pencils. Ask members to trace their family tree as creatively and quickly as possible, using first names and/or last names, plus their relationships to family members. Suggest as one possibility that they draw a tree, with the roots representing the parents and grandparents, and tree branches representing their siblings, children, and/or grandchildren.

After about five minutes, divide members into groups to discuss: **What family members left behind a spiritual legacy? What made their lives noteworthy? What impact has their legacy (or contribution) had on others who knew them or who were related to them? How would you like to be remembered by others who may follow in your footsteps?**

Say: **In this final chapter of the Book of Ruth, we can look back at her family tree and find an eternal legacy that she left behind. (See Matthew 1:5.) Today's lesson will help us analyze what preceded her lifetime impact.**

Discovering God's Principles *(25 minutes)*

Ask members to turn in their Bibles to Ruth 4:13-22. Discuss: **Who in this passage was impacted by Ruth's relationship to Boaz? What was her ultimate contribution to mankind?** (See Matthew 1:5, 16. She was part of the genealogy of Jesus Christ, Savior of the world.)

Instruct members to divide again into small groups. Be prepared to give them a brief overview of your study of the words "redeemer" and "redemption" and their use throughout Scripture. Then ask them to review from the text near the end of Section One both the comparisons and contrasts of Boaz to Christ. Discuss in small groups: **How was Ruth's legacy influenced by the actions of**

Boaz? How has our future been impacted by what Christ did for us?

In transition, point out that our ability to make a difference is due in large part to the difference Christ has made in our own lives. Distribute pencils and copies of Response Sheet 2.

Explain that these fifteen questions can serve to aid members in an inductive study of any Bible character, and that asking such questions can help us assess the final impact of a person's life. Ask the group to form five brainstorming groups, each group assigned Ruth's life. After about five to eight minutes, reassemble the group to report and support from Scripture (if possible) their conclusions.

Encourage members to select another character from the Book of Ruth to whom they might like to apply these fifteen questions.

Applying the Truth   *(25 minutes)*

MY COMMITMENT TO CHRIST

...To Have and to Hold...From This Day Forward...
(2 Corinthians 6:4-10)

1. For Better...   For Worse
2. For Richer...   For Poorer
3. In Sickness...   In Health

...Forsaking All Others...Till Death Do Us Part!
(2 Corinthians 11:23-29)

Visual Sketch 3
Our lives will count for Christ as we count the costs of our commitment.

Display Visual Sketch 3. Summarize: **In today's final episode, Boaz and Ruth are united in marriage, the ultimate in earthly commitments. There was also an implicit commitment to God in their relationship, a commitment that Ruth had declared early, even before marriage (Ruth 1:16-17). The traditional wedding vows spell out the costs of marital commitment, and just as there are costs in such a relationship, there are also costs in entering and maintaining a relationship with Christ.**

Ask group members to pair up, each partner looking up one of the two passages on Visual Sketch 3. Instruct them to look at what Paul's commitment to Christ cost him over time. Encourage them to match Paul's experiences with the traditional wedding vows. **Which of his experiences turned out for better? Which were for worse? Which were for richer? For poorer? Which cost him**

sickness? Point out that not all costs result in negative experiences. Ask: **What positive results came as a result of Paul's commitment?** Reassemble the group and ask: **How does the testimony and legacy Paul left behind inspire you to want a deeper commitment to Christ?**

In the last fifteen minutes, lead the group along with others you may have recruited through a candlelight Communion service. Here is a suggested format you may want to use or adapt:

- *Call to worship (Invite members to join together in celebrating Christ's commitment to us as the basis for leaving behind a lasting legacy.)*
- *Hymn or chorus about our redemption or Christ as our Redeemer*
- *Reading of 1 Corinthians 11:23-29*
- *Prayer of thanksgiving before the breaking of bread and its distribution*
- *Prayer of thanksgiving before partaking of the cup and its distribution*
- *Conversational prayers of commitment to becoming a lifelong difference-maker*
- *Closing hymn or chorus, such as "Take My Life."*

Alternate Ending:

If celebration of communion is inappropriate for your group, ask that people refer once again to the family tree they constructed in *Launching the Lesson*. Ask that they give sentence prayers of thanks, naming each person who has provided them with spiritual nurture. Then conduct a time of prayer where people whisper to God the names of those people to whom they would like to pass on their spiritual legacy.

Close your time of prayer with an appropriate praise or worship song.

ASSIGNMENT

1. Suggest that members practice using the questions on Response Sheet 2, applying them to another character in the Book of Ruth.
2. Tell members to read the prelude to Esther and chapter 5 of the text.

Session Five

THE QUEEN SAYS, "NO!"

TEXT, CHAPTER 5

Session Topic
God both rules and overrules, accomplishing all His purposes on earth.

Session Goals
1. To illustrate from daily life that God is not hiding, only hidden.
2. To discover from the lives of others in Scripture that God truly has the last word.
3. To evaluate opportunities in which members can become God's "gap" people.

Materials Needed
√ Bible
√ *Be Committed*
√ Recent newspapers and news magazines
√ World map
√ Bible map showing Esther's world
√ Poster board, marker
√ Blank paper, pencils

Special Preparation
1. Call to remind those who volunteered to do the special project in *Looking Ahead* in Session Two to be prepared to share a summary report during the "Body Life" section of this session.
2. At a local library, try to find a newspaper or year-end magazine article of the past two or three years that lists the year's top ten news items of the world. Be prepared to share some of your headlines in *Launching the Lesson*.

3. Look up the Book of Esther in a Bible encyclopedia or Bible dictionary to get the big picture of the book's content and main characters.

LESSON PLAN

Building the Body (5–8 minutes)

Introduce volunteer members who have agreed to five summary reports from the *Looking Ahead* section of Session Two. If there are questions of further interest in follow-up of ideas presented, encourage members to contact the presenters.

Launching the Lesson (10 minutes)

Distribute recent issues of newspapers and news magazines to members. Display a map of the world. Ask members to skim their news resources, looking for examples of God's presence and providence, even though His name may not be mentioned. Invite two or three members to peruse the world map looking for changes that may have occurred in the past five years due to changes in the political order. Then ask for members to share illustrations that God is present in our world and in control, listing their contributions on the poster board. Follow this by sharing your research on major world headlines, adding them to the poster board (especially graphic headlines about the downfall of communism and changes in major political boundaries).

Say: **As we move to the study on Esther, it may appear that God is in hiding. The truth is that He is merely hidden. He is alive and well in Esther's day, and also in our day.** Ask the group to pair up and answer this question: **What experiences have you had where at first God seemed silent, but later it became apparent that He was there all along?**

Tell the group that Jews in Esther's day probably experienced similar feelings as their very existence was threatened by those in power.

Discovering God's Principles (35 minutes)

Display the Bible map of Esther's world. Point out that the distance from Susa (Persian capital) to Jerusalem (Israel's capital) is approximately 600 miles, and that the Jews were in exile during the setting of this book. Say: **While it may appear politically that Persia was in control, God was still at work accomplishing His purposes, both in the lives of His people and in the secular world. Persia was a tool in God's hands to discipline His people while in exile. Also, God used His people to spread the news of the coming Messiah among those in Persia, a win-win situation for God and His purposes.**

Ask the group for three volunteers to role-play Ahasuerus (Xerxes) after his military defeat described by Wiersbe on page 75. Instruct these three to study together three of his weaknesses:

#1—His boastfulness (Esther 1:1-9)
#2—His drunkenness (1:10-12)
#3—His vindictiveness (1:13-22)

They may refer to both the biblical text and to Wiersbe's text as they prepare to present their weaknesses to a hypothetical support group. Those doing the role play should be prepared to answer:

■ *How did your weakness contribute to your downfall? With hindsight, what could you and would you have done differently? How did your demise prove that God was ultimately in control? What advice would you give to others beset with symptoms of pride?*

Then divide the other members into three groups, instructing them to look at the same passages and corresponding weaknesses, using the same resources. Ask them to brainstorm together how they might function as a support group to such a person. Ask:

■ *What similar personal examples could you offer to Ahasuerus to encourage him? As you prepare to listen to his testimony, what feedback would you give him?*

Urge them to be prepared to respond with biblical reasons as to how and why Xerxes might have gotten in this condition.

After the role-players and groups are prepared, ask each of the role-players to go to one of the support groups and tell his story, to be followed by the group's interaction and feedback.

Reassemble group members and say: **It is important that all in authority learn that all real authority comes from God, who is in complete control.** Ask for four volunteers to each role-play one of the four authorities below and to give a one minute testimony about how they learned this critical lesson:

#1 Pharaoh (Exodus 7:3-5)
#2 Nebuchadnezzar (Daniel 3–4)
#3 Belshazzar (Daniel 5)
#4 Herod Agrippa I (Acts 12:20-23)

While these volunteers have five minutes to prepare, encourage group members to skim these same passages, looking for clues to how they discovered that God is in first place. Then ask the volunteers to role-play their testimony before the group.

Applying the Truth *(15 minutes)*

Read Ezekiel 22:30 to the group. Affirm to members that God wants to use them to stand in the gap, just as He did Esther. Remind them of the author's quoting of a Grecian wise man, Pittacus, who said, "Know thine opportunities." On a poster board write and display Wiersbe's definition of opportunity: "A favorable occasion for grasping His appointment and accomplishing His purposes."

Distribute blank sheets of paper and pencils. Ask them to make three columns, headed by the words, "Needs," "Concerns," and "Desires." Instruct them to list as many opportunities as possible under each category that might represent an opportunity to accomplish God's purposes in their community, church, school, marketplace, or world. On the back side, urge them to list their spiritual gifts (if known) and personality strengths.

Instruct members to pair up to pray for one another as a prospective "gap" person.

ASSIGNMENT

1. Have everyone read chapter 6 of the text, thinking about evidences of God's hand at work in their lives.
2. Urge members to continue developing their opportunity list, and to ask a friend or two to confirm their assessment of their gifts and strengths.

Session Six

THE NEW QUEEN

TEXT, CHAPTER 6

Session Topic
God prepares His people to accomplish His work.

Session Goals
1. To illustrate how God precedes His people as He guides them.
2. To examine the doctrine of divine sovereignty in human affairs.
3. To pray for God's will to be done on earth as it is in heaven.

Materials Needed
√ Bible
√ *Be Committed*
√ Copies of Response Sheet 3, pencils
√ Poster board, marker

Special Preparation
1. Skim through the life of Joseph in Genesis 37, 39–44 and outline the key events or turning points of his life. Examine God's sovereignty in Genesis 45 and 50:15-21, and how His purposes prevailed over man's plans and preferences. What examples do you see that God is all-knowing and all-powerful?
2. Get an overview of the Book of Esther by reading the comments of Henrietta Mears in *What the Bible Is All About*.
3. Using a marker, print John 10:4 (NIV) in large letters on a sheet of poster board.

According to Dr. Kubler-Ross, the grief process has five stages:*

- **DENIAL**: The person feels that "this cannot be happening to me."
- **ANGER**: The sense of disbelief turns toward blaming oneself or others.
- **BARGAINING**: A person will think "if only" thoughts. A superficial sense of hope may develop.
- **DEPRESSION**: The person recognizes that real loss has occurred and that nothing can be done about it. The feeling of hopelessness and powerlessness to change anything can overwhelm.
- **ACCEPTANCE**: This involves submission to the new reality. A person is able to deal realistically with his or her new status in life.

EXERCISE: Pretend that you are a friend to Job or Naomi. You are hearing an unfolding story of trauma and grief and he or she asks you for feedback. What observations would you make about the stage he or she might be in? What encouragement could you give that might validate feelings and give perspective about the bigger picture of grief. Share with Job/Naomi your own experiences of handling grief. Remind them that grief is normal, necessary, and takes time. Explain that the order is not always predictable.

*Elisabeth Kubler-Ross, On Death and Dying (New York: Macmillan). Used by Permission.

Response Sheet 2 Use with session 4&7 of *Be Committed.*
© 1993 by SP Publications, Inc. Permission granted to purchaser to reproduce this Response Sheet for class p...

OPERATION DESERT STRENGTH
(Ephesians 6:10-18)

My desert helmet _____ (6:17)

My desert prayer _____ (6:18)

My desert breastplate _____ (6:14)

My desert shield _____ (6:16)

My desert sword _____ (6:17)

My desert belt _____ (6:14)

My desert boots _____ (6:15)

Response Sheet 4 Use with session 7 of *Be Committed*.
© 1993 by SP Publications, Inc. Permission granted to purchaser to reproduce this Response Sheet for class pur

3 After you were motivated, how did you use your influence to accomplish God's will? Describe any persistence that was required.

Esther 4:7-8, 12-14
Jonah 3:1-4

4 How did you see others being providentially prepared or used by God to accomplish His purposes?

Esther 4:14-17
Jonah 1:17; 3:5-6; 4:6-7

7 What results did you experience as a result of being proactive in pursuing God's will?

Esther 7:10; 8:11; 9:1; 10:1-3
Jonah 3:5-7

8 Who were the beneficiaries of your carrying out God's will?

Esther 9:1
Jonah 3:10; 4:11

Response Sheet 6 Use with session 10 of *Be Committed*.
© 1993 by SP Publications, Inc. Permission granted to purchaser to reproduce this Response Sheet for class pur

	Esther 6:1-5	Esther 6:6-10	Esther 6:11-14
Mordecai & Esther			
My Experience #1			
My Experience #2			

COUNTING THE COST... FINISHING THE COURSE
(Acts 20:24)

1	What did it cost you (actually or potentially) to follow God's will? Esther 4:11-14 Jonah 1-2	**2**	How did God motivate you to accomplish His purposes? How long did it take? Esther 3:15-4:1-3 Jonah 1:17; 3:1-4
5	In what ways did you sense God's timing? What part did man's free will fit into the picture? Esther 4:14-16 Jonah 1:17; 2:10; 4:6-7	**6**	How instrumental was your position or location in accomplishing God's will? Esther 5:1-7; 6:1-3 Jonah 3:1-3

Response Sheet 5 Use with session 8 of *Be Committed.*
© 1993 by SP Publications, Inc. Permission granted to purchaser to reproduce this Response Sheet for class pur

CHRIST'S "OPERATION DESERT STRENGTHS"

(Matthew 4:1-11; Luke 4:1-13)

What pieces of armor are evident in His battleground?
What strategies helped Him to stand?

1. _____
2. _____
3. _____
4. _____
5. _____

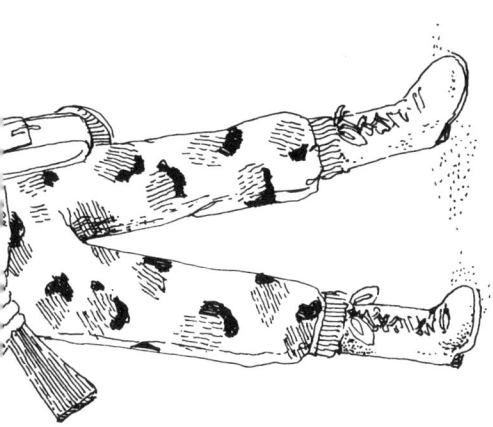

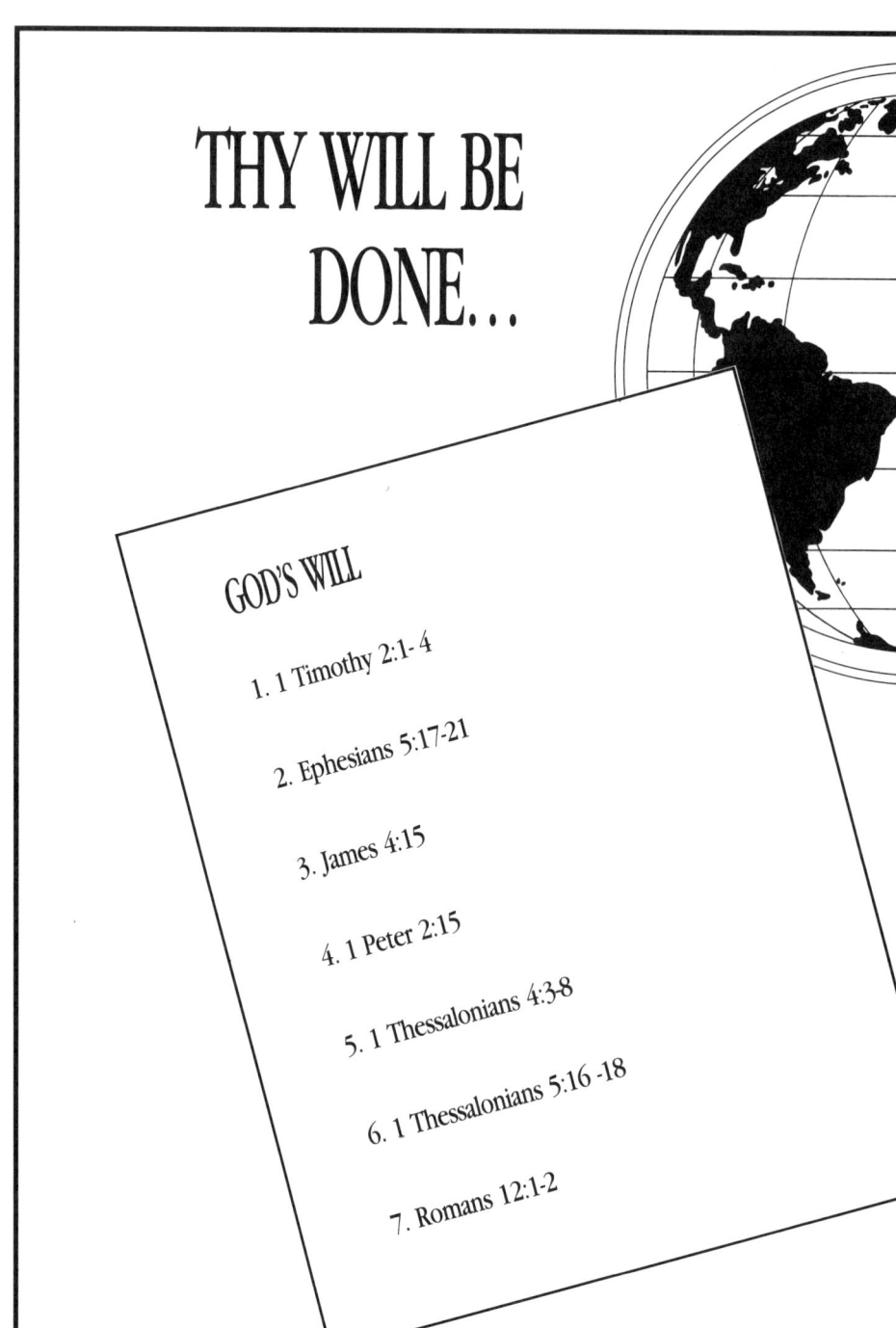

Response Sheet 3 Use with session 6 of *Be Committed*.
© 1993 by SP Publications, Inc. Permission granted to purchaser to reproduce this Response Sheet for class p

during the early ...?

4. Carefully attempt to determine the work which ... or she meet it?

5. What was the great crisis in this person's life, and how did he or her life?

6. What traits of character does this person display throughout his or ignoble? Did they help or hinder his or her life's work?

7. What friendships did the person have—were they noble or ignoble?

8. Determine, as far as possible, the influence this particular character had upon others, upon the nation, upon the history of religion.

9. What growth does the character of this person show?

10. Carefully determine the religious experiences of the character you are studying: prayer life, faith in God, service for God, knowledge of the Scriptures, courage in testimony, and attitude in worship.

11. What faults and shortcomings does Scripture reveal? What was the nature of the sin?

12. What, if any, was the great sin in this character's life? What effect did this sin have upon the future? What steps led to the sin? What effect and influence of this person's children?

13. What do you find to be the character and influence of this person is a type or antitype of Christ?

14. In what way do you think the character you are studying is a type or antitype of Christ?

15. What is one great lesson in this person's life for you?

(Wilbur M. Smith, *Profitable Bible Study*, Boston: W.A. Wilde Company, 1952: pp. 44-46.)

PERSIAN HISTORY

A GRIEF OBSERVED

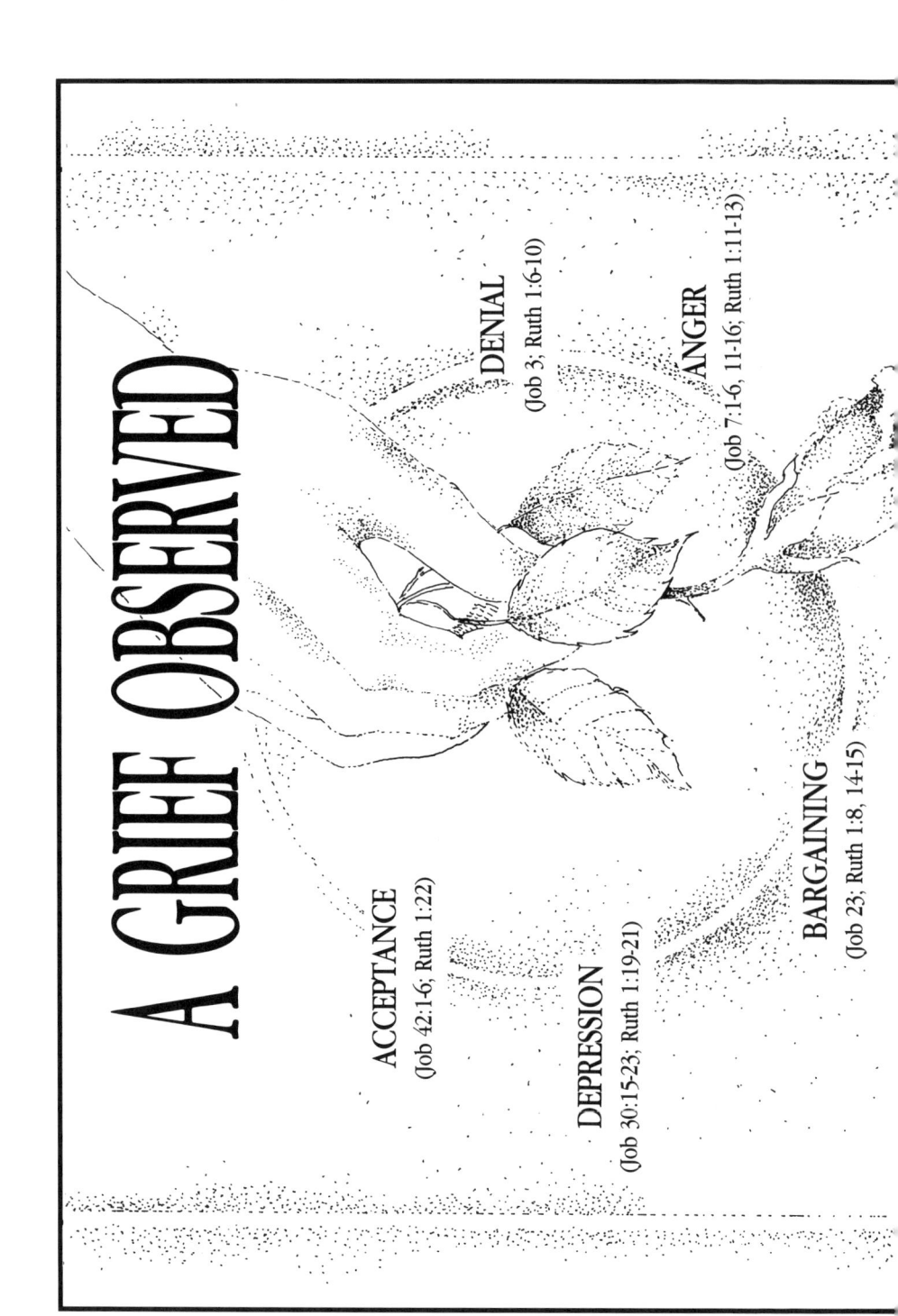

DENIAL
(Job 3; Ruth 1:6-10)

ANGER
(Job 7:1-6, 11-16; Ruth 1:11-13)

BARGAINING
(Job 23; Ruth 1:8, 14-15)

DEPRESSION
(Job 30:15-23; Ruth 1:19-21)

ACCEPTANCE
(Job 42:1-6; Ruth 1:22)

Response Sheet 1 Use with session 1 of *Be Committed*.
© 1993 by SP Publications, Inc. Permission granted to purchaser to reproduce this Response Sheet for class pur[poses]

LESSON PLAN

Launching the Lesson *(10–15 minutes)*

Display the poster board showing John 10:4. Lead the group in reading it in unison. Underline, "He goes on ahead of them." Tell about a time when the Lord went before you, provided for your needs, guided you, and protected you.

Divide the group into fours, encouraging them to share similar stories. After 8 minutes, reassemble the group and give a brief synopsis of Joseph's life as you studied it in the *Special Preparation*.

Discovering God's Principles *(35 minutes)*

Say: **God has given us free will and lets us experience the consequences of our choices. But He has the last word. In Esther 2, we see three examples of God's sovereignty, where He precedes His workers to accomplish His ultimate purposes.** Divide group members into three small groups. Assign each group one of the three sections below.

Group A — Esther 2:1-4 and Be Committed, *Chapter 6*
1. *What was the king's decision? What do you think motivated his decision?*
2. *What insight do you gain from Proverbs 21:1 about the limits of man's power? How did the king's decision accomplish God's purposes for His people?*
3. *Compare King Ahasuerus to King Cyrus in Isaiah 44:28–45:1-7. What does this tell you about whom God can use to accomplish His purposes? (He even uses nonbelievers.)*

Group B — Esther 2:5-18 and Be Committed, *Chapter 6*
1. *What were Mordecai's and Esther's realm of influence? Why do you think they concealed their identity as Jews?*
2. *While Mordecai's and Esther's lifestyle revealed that they were less than faithful to God's standards, both in marriage and other nonkosher behavior, God still overruled and accomplished His purposes. How can God do so without condoning their lifestyle?*
3. *What encouragement do we receive from 1 Timothy 1:13?*

Group C — Esther 2:19-23 and Be Committed, *Chapter 6*
1. *Do you feel that Mordecai was a "secret disciple" like Nicodemus,*

or was he simply neglecting to publicly honor God?
2. *How did he use his position for the good of the king? How was God's sovereignty at work behind the scenes?*
3. *Sometimes our acts of kindness are forgotten by men. What evidence is there in Joseph's life that God never forgets, and that His timing is always perfect? (Genesis 40:23; 41:1, 14; 45:5-8)*

Reassemble the group and quote writer Philip Yancey, "Faith is believing in advance what makes sense only in reverse." Say: **Faith requires that we believe in the sovereignty of God. The faithful in Hebrews 11 had little choice but to believe God in advance. Let's identify what would have made sense only in reverse about the following incidents:**

- *Noah—Hebrews 11:7* (That there really would be a flood and that the ark would protect them.)
- *Abraham—Hebrews 11:8-10* (The wisdom of God in leaving one's comfort zone for the unknown.)
- *Abraham—Hebrews 11:17-19* (The belief that God could raise Isaac from the dead.)
- *Moses' parents—Hebrews 11:23* (That God could actually save their child from harm's way.)

Applying the Truth *(10 minutes)*

Distribute pencils and copies of Response Sheet 3. Say: **The Lord's Prayer teaches us to pray that God's will would be done on earth as it is in heaven. In this session, we want to learn what His will is so that we can pray for it to be done.**

Ask people to pair up, look up the Scriptures on Response Sheet 3, and record their responses, plus specific prayer requests. Have them close by upholding each other in prayer.

ASSIGNMENT

1. Encourage members to pray daily through their Response Sheet 3 and add specific requests as they come to mind.
2. Tell members to read chapter 7 of the text as they are introduced to the third main character of this drama in Esther.

Looking Ahead

Invite a group volunteer to arrange a video showing of the movie *The Hiding Place* by Corrie ten Boom as an extra group activity that graphically illustrates the sovereignty of God.

Session Seven

AN OLD ENEMY WITH A NEW NAME

TEXT, CHAPTER 7

Session Topic
God is always stronger than our strongest enemies.

Session Goals
1. To become aware of the spiritual warfare that surrounds us.
2. To analyze spiritual battlegrounds and learn how to use them for spiritual victories.
3. To develop a proactive plan for managing spiritual warfare.

Materials Needed
√ Bible
√ *Be Committed*
√ Copies of Response Sheet 2, pencils
√ Copies of Response Sheet 4, pencils
√ Hymn books that have "A Mighty Fortress"
√ Poster board and marker

Special Preparation
1. Write in large print 1 John 4:4 on poster board with a marker.
2. Read Matthew 4:1-11 to see how Christ faced His (and our) enemy, Satan. Then read Ephesians 6:10-18 to see the resources given us with which to face the enemy of our souls.
3. Clip examples of evil influence from news articles, advertising, business reports, articles about leisure, abusive behavior, addictions, cults, pictures of unbiblical relationships, excess materialism, occult, or deception of any kind. Bring these to give the group a greater awareness of spiritual warfare in their lives and culture.

41

LESSON PLAN

Launching the Lesson *(5–10 minutes)*

Pass out the cultural examples from *Special Preparation* that give hints of spiritual warfare in our culture. Ask: **What does your news article or advertisement highlight as a potential area of conflict for Christians?**

Read 1 John 2:15-17 and ask: **How would you categorize the clipping you hold — the cravings of sinful man, the lust of his eyes, or the boasting of what he has and does?**

Read James 1:13-15; 4:1-3. Ask: **In addition to outward contributions to inward conflict, what other causes are there for inward conflict based on these verses?** Say: **In today's session we will look for hope and help in our spiritual battlegrounds. Our first step has been to acknowledge that such a conflict exists. And that is half the battle.**

Discovering God's Principles *(30–35 minutes)*

Say: **In Esther, we see an example of earthly conflict in which there are forces at work to destroy God's people and thus thwart His plans to bring in His Son, the Messiah.**

Distribute again copies of Response Sheet 2 and pencils. Ask members to use the Wiersbe text plus various Scripture references from Esther to discuss the following questions applied to the villain Haman: 2, 6, 7, 9, 11, 12, 14, and 15.

Divide into small groups. Half of the groups should brainstorm the first four questions, and the remaining groups should interact on the last four assigned questions. After about 10 minutes, ask a reporter from each group to summarize their conclusions.

Say: **God's enemies have opposed God's people throughout history, whether Haman, Herod, or Hitler. What lesson on spiritual warfare have you learned from the life of Haman, even though he was a negative example?**

Say: **As groups, I want you to choose one of the three following Bible characters, skim the Bible passage, and compare or contrast your choice to Haman as a character.** Instruct them to discuss: **What conflict did this character face? How did he handle his conflict** (by using spiritual principles or by neglecting spiritual principles)? Give examples of your conclusions:

   #1 — Saul and the Amalekites (1 Samuel 15)
   #2 — David and Goliath (1 Samuel 17)

#3—Daniel in the lions' den (Daniel 6)

After about 10 minutes, reassemble members and ask a volunteer from each group to distill from either a negative or positive example a principle for spiritual warfare. For instance, with Saul: incomplete obedience is still disobedience (1 Samuel 15:18-19); David: the battle is the Lord's and He is the explanation for any victories, not our weapons of warfare (1 Samuel 17:47); Daniel: consistent prayer is the secret of deliverance (Daniel 6:10-11).

Read 1 Corinthians 10:6-12. Remind the group that we can learn from Bible characters, whether positive or negative examples, about how to live victorious, Christlike lives.

Applying the Truth *(20 minutes)*

Distribute copies of Response Sheet 4 and pencils. Say: **In Ephesians 6:10-18, we have the key weapons, both defensive and offensive, for effective spiritual warfare.** Ask members to pair up.

Write on your sheets:
— The value of each piece of armor.
— Count how many times the word "stand" appears.
— How does the word "stand" relate to the goal of our spiritual warfare? (6:13)
— What use of this spiritual armor did Christ use in His own temptation?

Discuss with your neighbor:
— Which pieces of armor come easiest for you?
— Which represent areas of neglect and require more work for you?
— How would you like to be more active in fighting the spiritual war this week?
— Pray with your neighbor about this section.

Display a copy of 1 John 4:4 that you wrote on the poster board as a symbol of hope as they fight the good fight of faith.

Close the session by distributing hymn books and singing together the hymn, "A Mighty Fortress."

ASSIGNMENT

1. Encourage members to memorize 1 John 4:4 this week.
2. Have members read chapter 8 of the text and ask themselves, "What evidences do I see of God's control in my life?"

Session Eight

A DAY OF DECISION

TEXT, CHAPTER 8

Session Topic
Commitment involves counting the costs of doing God's will and then following through.

Session Goals
1. To examine contemporary examples of commitment to excellence.
2. To analyze biblical models of those who counted the costs of doing God's will.
3. To explore getting involved with those who are perishing.

Materials Needed
√ Bible
√ *Be Committed*
√ Recording of one of these songs: "Find Us Faithful" (Steve Green, *Find Us Faithful,* Sparrow); "Take Up Your Cross" (Ray Boltz, *Another Child to Hold,* Spectra); "Who Will Stand in the Gap," (Scott Wesley Brown, *The Passionate Pursuit,* Word); CD or tape player
√ Note cards, pencils; poster board, markers
√ Copies of Response Sheet 5, pencils, scissors

Special Preparation
1. Use a marker to write in large letters on the poster board this quote from the text by Edmund Burke: "All that is required for evil to triumph is for good men to do nothing."
2. Talk with your pastor or the chairperson of your missions committee to learn what kind of opportunities exist in your commu-

nity for reaching out to those in need (rescue missions, the homeless, AIDS patients, crisis pregnancy centers, or abortion protests).
3. For *Launching the Lesson,* gather purpose statements from businesses or schools to discover the costs these people pay to accomplish their objectives. Also survey *In Search of Excellence* by Thomas J. Peters and Robert J. Waterman, Jr. (Harper and Row, 1982) with the same goal. Prepare to share your findings.

LESSON PLAN

Launching the Lesson *(10 minutes)*

Say: **Secular businesses have been discovering the secret to success—high commitment to high standards to reach a high goal. They appear willing to pay almost any price to advance their cause, whether in products or services.** Share with the group some of your findings from books on business and purpose statements. Ask: **What evidence is there that successful companies count the costs of success (or failure)? What is their bottom-line motivation?** (Often increased profits)

Then display the Edmund Burke quote. Say: **If Christians are to make a difference in the world, we too will need a high degree of commitment. Moreover, we have an even higher cause: the Lord Jesus Christ—knowing Him and making Him known. According to this quote, however, failure to make such a commitment can have disastrous results.** Ask: **What examples from history can you cite that would prove the truth of Edmund Burke's conclusion? What examples from culture can you point to that show the rewards of commitment?** (Athletics, academics, politics, finance, science, music, art)

Discovering God's Principles *(35 minutes)*

Say: **In addition to cultural models of cost-counting, it is even more essential to have biblical models. Today, we will look at both a positive and negative role model. From negative examples we will find that even if we are uncooperative, God can overrule us to accomplish His will. We will analyze Mordecai as a positive example and Jonah as a negative one.**

Divide members into two groups, and distribute to each member a copy of Response Sheet 3, pencils, and a pair of scissors to each group. Ask a group leader for each group to cut up the eight squares, shuffle them, and give each member at least one card. Tell Group A to answer the questions using Mordecai as a positive role model. Ask Group B to answer the questions using Jonah as a negative example. Both groups can refer to the Scripture references on their cards to gain insights on doing God's will.

Ask each card-bearer to spend 3 to 5 minutes answering his or her question, making notes on the back of the card. (References may not suggest an explicit answer. They should feel free to analyze the content and record their ideas.) Then for the next 20 minutes, ask each card-bearer in numerical order to share conclusions and to ask for additional insights from fellow members.

Reassemble members and discuss: **What general principle for following and following through on God's will did you learn? What lessons are there to emulate or to avoid?**

Ask a volunteer to read Luke 14:25-33 about counting the costs of following Jesus. Discuss the evidence that Jesus counted the costs of doing the Father's will (Luke 22:41-42). What example did Christ set for us when He did His Father's will? (Hebrews 12:2-3)

Applying the Truth *(15 minutes)*

Say: **Like Esther and Mordecai, we too make a difference in our world. Sometimes the stakes are high, the costs great, and the unknowns intimidating.** Read Proverbs 24:11-12 and emphasize the potential risk of remaining neutral or silent.

Ask members to brainstorm in groups of three or four potential outreach possibilities in their community. Record their resources on blank poster board.

Distribute note cards and pencils. Ask people to list three viable opportunities for which they have burdens, passions, or experiences. Urge them to rank them in order of preference.

Prayerfully listen to one of the songs listed in *Materials Needed*.

ASSIGNMENT

1. Urge members to make phone or personal contact this week about one item on their cards. Encourage them to make notes about what involvement might cost in time, money, and other commitment.
2. Read chapter 9 of the text. Bring a clipping of a contemporary scandal as suggested by the opening paragraph.

Session Nine

A DAY IN THE LIFE OF THE PRIME MINISTER

TEXT, CHAPTER 9

Session Topic
Praying and working for change are part of the price of our commitment to do God's will.

Session Goals
1. To be convinced from contemporary examples that sin backfires on the sinner.
2. To discuss the importance of balancing work and prayer in doing God's will.
3. To develop a strategy for praying for revival.

Materials Needed
√ Bible
√ *Be Committed*
√ Poster board, markers
√ 10 note cards per member, pencils
√ Equipment for a video presentation (optional)

Special Preparation
1. Gather news clippings illustrating that our sins will find us out, and that the wrong we do to others, we do to ourselves. Videotape news highlights that also illustrate these truths.
2. Prepare for *Applying the Truth* by making your own file of biblical prayer promises, character incentives, and other categories that may motivate you toward personal revival and prayer for local and worldwide revivals. Record relevant Scripture verses on note cards. Prepare to share what changes you notice in your own heart as you daily review and meditate on these Scriptures.

LESSON PLAN

Launching the Lesson (10–12 minutes)

Invite those who brought news clippings of contemporary scandals to share a summary of each article. Say: **The point of the exercise is not to satisfy our curiosity for such news stories, but to show the trustworthy nature of biblical principles that our sins will find us out.** As Wiersbe points out, "The wrong we do to others, we do to ourselves." Then show the optional video that you prepared according to instructions in *Special Preparation*.

Read Ecclesiastes 8:14. Comment that this verse refers to the irony that "good things sometimes happen to bad people" while "bad things sometimes happen to good people." Ask: **How does this square with God's principles that our sins find us out?** (Refer members back to verses 12 and 13 which put the irony against the backdrop of the big picture.) Conclude this section by pointing to the text which focuses on Haman's downfall and the steps that got him there.

Discovering God's Principles (35 minutes)

Say: **Our objective will be to find the balance of work and prayer in doing God's will. Some of us may be inclined to be "doers," and we need to balance out our doing with praying. Others of us may find it easier to pray, but difficult to "put legs to our prayers," and that is where we need balance. As we look at the actions of Esther and Mordecai in doing God's will, we'll see a balance of working and praying to accomplish God's will.**

Instruct members to pair up and read Esther 4:1-5, 15-17, and have them discuss: **What precipitated this fervor in prayer and fasting? Do you think that crises are the usual way we are motivated to seek God?** Ask them to exchange personal examples of what motivates them to pray.

Then ask them to look at Esther 5 to find examples of how Esther also "put legs to her prayers," and to look at Esther 4 to find Mordecai busy planning strategies. Have them follow up their findings by reading Proverbs 16:9. Ask: **How are man's plans balanced by God's interventions?**

Encourage members to look at Joshua's model in Joshua 7, examining this passage in groups of four. Ask: **What evidence was there that Joshua was a doer? What evidence that he was a pray-er? In verses 6-9, it appears Joshua's prayer time is a spiritual activity, but the Lord rebukes him by telling him it's a time to act. Discuss: **What does Joshua's example tell us about the timing of prayer and work and the need for balance in our lives. Might prayer be an excuse for not acting? Might work be presumptuous if we do not seek God?** Encourage them to scan Joshua 9 to see that failure to seek God was equally disastrous in their desire to do God's will.

Suggest to the whole group other possible areas of needed balance. For instance, we must balance the gifts of the Spirit with the fruit of the Spirit (Galatians 5:22-23). As we serve the Lord, we need to develop character so that our gifts truly reflect Christ. Scripture also refers to a balance between faith and works.

Ask the groups of four to read James 2:14-26 which emphasizes that "faith without works is dead." Have them brainstorm: **How did Abraham's faith and actions work together?** (Refer them to Hebrews 11:8-11.) **How might he have neglected one or the other? What do you think would have been the consequence?**

Now have members return to their original pairs. Say: **Find evidences in Esther 5 of Esther's faith, and evidences of her works. Looking ahead to chapters 6 and 7, how did God reward her faith and works? What risks did both she and Mordecai take to step out in faith and act? Share examples of how you have taken risks to step out in faith and to do God's will. What rewards have you experienced?**

Applying the Truth *(15 minutes)*

Say: **Just as Mordecai and Esther had a burden for their times and their people and their world, so it is likely that we too want to see our world changed. Perhaps we can envision those changes starting within our churches or within ourselves. Let's resolve to pray for the revival of ourselves, our churches, and our world. Let's develop strong convictions from God's Word.**

Then, share your experiences since last session from *Special Preparation,* how exploring God's truths and promises has motivated you to pray. Show them your prayer card file and the categories you have developed for daily review. Distribute 10 note cards and a pencil to each member, and ask them to select one of the following categories in which to begin collecting appropriate Scriptures:

Promises on Prayer
Truths about God's Sovereignty
Truths about Man's Need for God
Other

Then urge them to skim the Wiersbe text looking for verses they could jot down on a single card for daily review. For instance, under the category, *Promises on Prayer,* the following verses are appropriate: 2 Chronicles 7:14; Mark 11:22-25; John 16:24. (Record both verse and reference.)

Using a poster board and marker, place the following three categories before the group:

Personal revival
Church-wide revival
Worldwide revival

Ask members in pairs to brainstorm how they could begin to pray specifically for revival in each of the three categories.

Urge them to close in conversational prayer, praying sentence prayers for each category of revival, or praying through the Scriptures as they have recorded them on their note cards.

ASSIGNMENT

1. Encourage members to add more verse cards to their collection each week and review them in daily prayer.
2. Ask them to read chapter 10 of the text.

Looking Ahead
1. Ask for three or four volunteers to read *Daughters of the Church* by Ruth Tucker and Walter Liefeld and together form a panel to discuss the role of Christian women in leadership and ministry—especially in light of Esther's obvious gifts, roles, and opportunities. Ask a couple of other volunteers to take a poll of questions that panelists will discuss during Session 12.
2. An alternative plan for Session 13 might be to have a guest speaker from a local synagogue come and conduct a sample "Feast of Purim," walking your group through its historical significance to the Book of Esther. That person may suggest additional preparations your members might make to make it more authentic.

Session Ten

WARNING SIGNALS

TEXT, CHAPTER 10

Session Topic
Committed Christians are likely to see God's hand of providence in their lives.

Session Goals
1. To explain God's "delays."
2. To identify God's good hand of providence in the lives of others.
3. To praise God for His providence in our lives.

Materials Needed
√ Bible
√ *Be Committed*
√ Copies of Response Sheet 6, pencils
√ Paper, pencils, poster board, multicolored markers
√ Hymn books or chorus books for each member

Special Preparation
1. Prior to the session, use a sheet of paper and make a list or time line of all the major and secondary events as you skim through the Book of Esther. Place arrows above the events that reveal God's providence in circumstances, timing, or source people.
2. On Response Sheet 6, record a couple of your experiences of God's providence where His timing and orchestration of events showed that "all things work together for good" to those who are committed to His purposes.
3. Obtain a copy of the book *The Seven Habits of Highly Effective People* by Stephen R. Covey, Simon and Schuster, 1989. Review

the seven principles of personal leadership or delegate this to a volunteer group member. Assess how many of these principles were used by Mordecai and Esther. (You will use this project again in Session 11.)
4. Look up and read the entry on "Providence" in *The New Bible Dictionary,* J.D. Douglas, editor.

LESSON PLAN

Building the Body (5 minutes)

Ask members to recall their experiences this past week of praying for revival and meditating on their selected Scriptures. If your group is large, divide members into smaller groups for sharing. Be sure to participate yourself. Ask: **How did meditating on Scripture impact your prayer times? Has your passion to pray for revival intensified since our last session?**

Launching the Lesson (15 minutes)

Say: **The author's quote, "God's delays are not God's denials," sounds great but may not always feel that way to us. Think back on an experience where you encountered a delay from God. What kind of explanations for that delay went through your mind?** Possible responses may include the following:
- *"I felt like God didn't care."*
- *"I felt like God was in hiding."*
- *"I felt grief due to what appeared to be a 'No!' to my inquiries."*
- *"I wondered what was wrong with me, or my walk with God!"*
- *"I wondered if my request of Him was somehow selfish."*
- *"I wondered if I'd failed to meet some of His criteria for doing His will."*

Ask: **With the hindsight you now have, what are your explanations for those delays?** Review the story of Lazarus' sickness and death (John 11:1-44) and how his sisters reacted to Christ's delay. Ask: **How did Christ's delay actually work for good? How was it a win-win situation in the end?**

Discovering God's Principles (30 minutes)

Distribute blank paper and pencils to members and ask them to form groups of four or five. Instruct them to each take two chapters of Esther until the entire book is covered. Have them skim those chapters looking for key and secondary events in the unfolding drama that they might put on a time line. Then have each person, with the help of fellow members, construct a time line of events in the Book of Esther. When finished, instruct them to discuss where they would place arrows above events that, in retrospect, point to the providence of God (His timing, His networking, etc.).

Reassemble members and ask each group to present its time line and to point out the arrows they placed above key events or delays. Record on poster board using multicolored markers a combined time line along with observations about God's providence. Ask: **As for Haman, how could those delays have worked for his good had he been responsive to God?** (See Ezekiel 33:11 and 2 Peter 3:9.) **How does our free will mesh with God's providence?** (See Matthew 23:37.)

Distribute copies of Response Sheet 6. Say: **Moses experienced at least 10 delays from Pharaoh before God's delivered His people from Egypt. Hebrews 11:27b gives the secret to his endurance. "He persevered because he saw him who is invisible." If we are to persevere, we must identify God's good hand of providence in our lives. We must look beyond delays and trust His ultimate purposes. One way to strengthen that perspective is to look back on the lives of others who had to walk by faith and not by sight, just as we now have to walk.**

Instruct members to form three teams, each team selecting two of the three examples. Ask them to record their observations about what they saw under each category that would help them see God's providence, whether in circumstances, timing, or God's network of people. Reassemble members and review briefly what groups saw and learned from the Bible characters. Now ask members to pair up and privately record two of their own experiences on Response Sheet 6. When finished ask them to exchange one story with each other.

Applying the Truth *(15 minutes)*

Say: **Reviewing God's providence in the lives of others and in our own lives can only make us want to praise and thank Him for the great God that He is. Let us practice praising God for His providence, in song, Scripture reading, and praise prayers.**

Distribute copies of hymn or chorus books and ask members to select praise songs for the group to sing that would remind us all of His providence. Some examples might include, "Great Is Thy Faithfulness," "How Great Thou Art," and "God Moves in a Mysterious Way." If song selections have an unfamiliar tune, have the group read the stanzas instead. Ask for three volunteers to read the following Scriptures and for three others to follow them with praise appropriate to the verses: Psalm 33:10-11, Proverbs 21:30, Romans 8:31.

Continue the pattern of Scripture reading, prayer praise, and song until time runs out. Close with conversational prayer in pairs, thanking God for His providence.

ASSIGNMENT

1. Remind those who volunteered last session to read *Daughters of the Church* plus those who volunteered to prepare questions for panelists to continue to get ready for their presentation in Session 12.
2. Delegate the reading of *The Seven Habits of Highly Effective People* as described in the *Special Preparation* section of today's session.
3. Have members read chapter 11 of the text.

Session Eleven

THE MASK COMES OFF

TEXT, CHAPTER 11

Session Topic
God's law of sowing and reaping applies both to believers and unbelievers.

Session Goals
1. To examine the habits of highly effective people.
2. To illustrate the law of sowing and reaping, both positively and negatively.
3. To identify masks that make us ineffective as God's servants.

Materials Needed
√ Bible
√ *Be Committed*
√ Poster board, markers for the group
√ Visual Sketch 4
√ Packs of 3-M Post-its with a role on each one for *Applying the Truth*

Special Preparation
1. If you are using *The Seven Habits of Highly Effective People* by Stephen R. Covey, list the seven habits on poster board with a one-sentence definition or description of each. As you review these habits, try to think through which of the ones Esther and Mordecai may have applied. If the book is not available, look for substitutes on management and leadership principles. Examples: *Leadership* by Calvin Miller, Navpress, 1987; *Leaders* by Warren Bennis and Bert Nanus, Harper and Row, 1985; *13 Fatal Errors Managers Make* by W. Steven Brown, Fleming H.

Revell Company, 1985; *Bringing Out the Best in People* by Alan Loy McGinnis, Augsburg Publishing House, 1985.
2. To prepare for *Applying the Truth,* try to get a copy of *Adult Children: The Secrets of Dysfunctional Families* by John and Linda Friel, Health Communications, Inc., or an equivalent that addresses the many roles that people play in a family. Notice the masks that we wear: doer, enabler, scapegoat, and so on. Try to think of contemporary masks Christians often wear that may make us ineffective—perfectionism, for example.
3. Reproduce Visual Sketch 4 on poster board.

LESSON PLAN

Launching the Lesson *(15 minutes)*

Introduce the member (if a volunteer has agreed to do this) who will present the book *The Seven Habits of Highly Effective People* or an equivalent book). Display the seven habits (or their equivalent) on poster board along with their one-sentence descriptions. After they are presented, ask the group to reflect on the main characters—Esther and Mordecai—and brainstorm about which of those habits or principles would apply to their leadership style. For instance, how proactive were Esther and Mordecai toward their predicament and opportunities? How did they use the habit of interdependence? How did their thinking reflect a win-win strategy?

Then help the group think through why Haman was ineffective in his leadership role. Ask: **Which of these habits or principles did Haman fail to cultivate? What wrong assumptions did he make?** (That he was somehow safe since he had experienced no consequences.)

Discovering God's Principles *(30 minutes)*

Introduce the universal principle found in Galatians 6:7-8, as it applies to both believers and unbelievers: we reap what we sow. Say: **While this principle is true, it is often misconstrued to apply only to negative sowing and reaping. We'll soon see in Scripture, however, that there can be positive sowing and reaping as well. We'll begin with some negative examples, and move on to some positive ones.**

Instruct members to skim through the Wiersbe text, chapter 11, and anywhere in the Book of Esther, for some of the misdeeds that Haman sowed. Then ask members to share their observations as you record them on a poster board.

Say: **The author suggested in the previous chapter that Haman suffered the difference between reputation and character. While famous for his reputation, which depended on his office, his wealth, and his authority, he lacked character. The tragedy is that his reputation was easily taken from him.** Ask: **What deficiencies of character have you sensed about Haman? What evidence would you cite?** (His boastfulness, failure to take advice, pride, scheming of conspiracies, malice)

	SOWING	REAPING
NEGATIVE	1. Jacob (Genesis 27:1-29) 2. Pharoah (Exodus 1:15-16) 3. David (2 Samuel 11)	1. Genesis 37:31-35 2. Exodus 14:26-28 3. 2 Samuel 16:20-23
POSITIVE	1. Matthew 10:42 2. Matthew 25:31-46 3. Romans 6:3-4	1. Matthew 10:42 2. Matthew 25:31-46 3. Romans 6:3-4

Visual Sketch 4
It is important for us to see both the positive and negative examples of sowing and reaping.

Now display Visual Sketch 4 and divide group members into two teams to illustrate from Scripture other examples of this universal law. One team should be instructed to research the negative examples, while the other team explores the positive ones. Encourage each team to divide up the research, then after recording their observations, report to their teammates. Make sure that each team has a poster board and marker to record their results.

Here are some possible results.

#1—Jacob: kills an animal and lies to his father; later his sons kill an animal and lie to him.

#2—Pharaoh: gives orders to drown the Jewish baby boys; eventually, his army was drowned in the Red Sea.

#3—David: secretly took his neighbor's wife and committed adultery; his son Absalom took his father's concubines and openly committed adultery with them.

Reassemble members and have each team share their illustrations of the principles of sowing and reaping. Ask: **What positive contemporary examples have you seen or experienced that would verify this principle?**

Applying the Truth *(15 minutes)*

Say: **Unlike Haman, we don't want to wear masks of reputation that are devoid of character.** In our day, counselors are identifying many roles played out in dysfunctional family behavior, roles that often mask our true feelings, and ones that make us ineffective as God's servants.

Point out some of these roles or masks as found in the book *Adult Children,* mentioned in *Special Preparation.* Distribute a role recorded on a 3-M Post-it Note to each member. Depending on the group's size, some members may have duplicate roles. After a brief description of each role, divide members into groups of four, asking each one to role play his or her role as written on the 3-M Post-it Note. Have the person role-playing pretend he or she is talking to another person on a telephone while the three group members listen in. Their role is to guess what mask the "talker" is wearing. Have members take turns role-playing until all have.

Reassemble members and read Ephesians 4:17-32, pointing out that with authentic Christianity we can focus on developing Christ-like character, not mere reputation. Say: **As Christians, we don't have to play unhealthy roles or wear masks that hide our pain or areas of vulnerability. We can speak the truth in love to one another, grow up into Christ, and increase our effectiveness in His service.**

Encourage members to pair up and pray for one another as together we seek to become authentic servants of Christ.

ASSIGNMENT

1. For those who may wish to further explore the subject matter in *Applying the Truth*, recommend the book *Toxic Faith* by Stephen Arterburn and Jack Felton, Oliver Nelson, 1991, a book which helps people take off religious masks as they come to understand them.
2. Ask members to read chapter 12 of the text.
3. Again remind the panelists and emcees to be ready with their book review and discussion of women in ministry and leadership.

Session Twelve

FROM VICTIMS TO VICTORS

TEXT, CHAPTER 12

Session Topic
Commitment involves using our influence and resources to accomplish God's purposes.

Session Goals
1. To examine the role of women in ministry and leadership.
2. To discover ways that others have used their influence to accomplish God's purposes.
3. To evaluate our potential influence on our world.

Materials Needed
√ Bible
√ *Be Committed*
√ Poster board, markers, paper, pencils
√ Hymn books with the song, "So Send I You"

Special Preparation
1. Remind panelists to prepare their discussion of key issues surrounding women in ministry and leadership. They should plan 15 minutes to share insights gained from *Daughters of the Church* by Ruth Tucker and Walter Liefeld. They should also respond to questions brewing among group members. Remind panelists that the issue of women in ministry and leadership (lay and professional) is a sensitive topic among Christians. They should assume that all Christians will not agree on this topic. Let them know that it's okay to say, "I don't know."
2. Prepare a poster board with categories for the resume and job description described in *Applying the Truth*.

LESSON PLAN

Launching the Lesson *(20 minutes)*

Introduce this session's panelists who will present material mentioned in *Special Preparation* on the topic of women in leadership and ministry. After about 15 minutes, thank them for their hard work on a difficult subject.

In transition, say: **Scripture shows women playing strategic roles in accomplishing God's purposes to advance the Gospel. Esther and Ruth are prime Old Testament examples. In the New Testament, we find women playing a key role in Christ's ministry as well as in Paul's.** Ask: **What significant changes for women do you hear announced in Peter's Pentecost message in Acts 2:17-18? If you were a woman in Paul's day reading Galatians 3:26-29, what might be your response? What are the implications of 1 Peter 3:7 for husbands and wives?**

Discovering God's Principles *(15 minutes)*

Say: **During the past sessions, we've seen how Mordecai and Esther have used their influence to save the lives of fellow Jews. Today, we will continue to look at how they used their positions to intercede on behalf of others. Our goal is to learn how God can use us to intercede for our own generation.**

Divide members into groups of five and appoint leaders. Give groups poster board and markers. Instruct them to use the Wiersbe text plus Esther 8 to devise a strategy to spare their fellow Jews, recording their strategy on the poster board in a graphic rendering. Ask the group to see themselves as a think tank, identifying key players, strategic moves, follow-up activities, and so forth. After 10 minutes, ask appointed leaders to share their group's strategy.

Emphasize that doing God's will is a team effort. Esther couldn't do everything, but she could do something. Like Esther, we need to do what we can to reach out to our generation.

Applying the Truth *(25 minutes)*

Display two poster boards that list the following categories: Poster board #1 *Résumé:* My Past Experiences, My Past Accomplishments, References. Poster board #2 *Job Description:* Position or Title I Desire, Responsibilities I Could Envision, People I'd Be Responsible For or To, People I Would Work With, Spiritual Gifts and Skills I Would Need, My Personality, My Passion, My Network of People and Resources.

Distribute copies of blank paper and pencils. Instruct members on one side of their paper to write a résumé of their past track record in influencing others, whether at home, in the marketplace, at school, at church, and so on. Ask them to select what they feel has been their most significant contribution to the cause of Christ in their generation.

As they finish, challenge them with: **If resources were not an obstacle, what influence would you like to have to help change your world for Christ?** Then as people to write on the other side of the paper their own job description for that position of influence. Encourage them to think through how their spiritual gifts, their personality strengths, and their passions might blend together to make an impact. Ask them to think: **Who might be on my team? Who would I really like to reach** (example: the homeless, singles, latchkey children, blended families, international students)**? What are the possibilities that my dreams could come true?** Urge members to pair up and share their job descriptions.

Distribute hymn books and invite members to prayerfully sing "So Send I You" or an equivalent hymn or chorus.

ASSIGNMENT

1. Ask for volunteers to assist a guest speaker with the closing session's celebration of the Feast of Purim, providing needed elements for atmosphere or leading in assigned activities.
2. Invite members to prepare to share the most important thing God taught them through this study and how He used the weekly interactions and assignments to help them become more committed.
3. Instruct members to read Wiersbe's chapter 13, and then review the Book of Esther. Challenge them to arrange Esther like a three-act play. What titles would they give each act? What title would they give to this historic drama?

Session Thirteen

GOD KEEPS HIS PROMISES

TEXT, CHAPTER 13

Session Topic
Commitment is God coming through for His people, and His people coming through for Him.

Session Goals
1. To celebrate God's coming through for His people.
2. To examine the biblical basis for celebrating every spiritual blessing.
3. To evaluate our growth in commitment to the Lord and to His will.

Materials Needed
√ Bible
√ *Be Committed*
√ Paper, pencils for the group
√ Hymn books or chorus books
√ Poster board, markers

Special Preparation
1. Be sure to connect with your guest speaker and your group volunteers to coordinate a celebration of the Feast of Purim. As you interact with your guest speaker (ideally one with a Jewish background who understands this feast and can walk others through it), make a checklist of needed supplies plus an order of service.
2. Look up "Purim" in *The New Bible Dictionary* to enhance your own understanding of this feast. If no speaker is available, be prepared to give a brief background sketch of this feast as it relates to the Book of Esther.

3. Be prepared to share what you have gained through these two historic dramas illustrating true commitment. Answer for yourself, How have I become more committed as a result of this study?

LESSON PLAN

Building the Body *(8–10 minutes)*

Ask members to share some of the important things they have learned about commitment as a result of their group interactions and assignments.

Launching the Lesson *(30–50 minutes)*

Introduce your guest speaker and emcee for the Feast of Purim celebration. This event may actually take the entire session. If this event is not possible, then substitute your own preparation on this subject mentioned in the *Special Preparation* section, giving the group a historical overview of how this feast has been celebrated in the past. Then solicit ideas from the group about how they might celebrate their own personal Feast of Purim and how it might reflect a way that God has rescued them. Perhaps you could encourage a few testimonies in that regard interspersed with hymns or choruses from the song books you have on hand.

Discovering God's Principles *(20 minutes)*

Distribute paper and pencils to members. Challenge them to arrange the Book of Esther into individual acts as you might for a drama. Instruct them to use the Book of Esther to look for major divisions in this unfolding drama. Then ask them to give titles to each act and a creative title for the entire book as a means of quick review. Ask members to come together in groups of three to share their titles and how they arrived at them.

Then ask the groups to skim Esther 9:1-17 to look at the basis for celebration and 9:18-32, the actual Feast of Purim. Have them discuss: **What was the general cause for celebration?** (God's deliverance of the Jews, their triumph over their enemies) **In the second part of Esther 9, how did the Jews specifically celebrate this victory?** (Feasting, giving presents, giving away food, gifts to the poor) **What would be the point of making this a perennial** feast? What celebrations do Christians observe? What cause do we have for celebrating as believers? (1 Corinthians 11:23-26) Say: **One of the motivations for our commitment to Christ is that of celebrating His commitment to us. As Christians, let's find even more opportunities to celebrate every blessing He bestows on us.**

Applying the Truth *(15 minutes)*

Draw a fuel gauge on poster board, placing the word EMPTY on one end of the gauge and FULL on the other end of the gauge. Display this poster and a blank poster board to write on. Say: **I hope that our time together has helped increase our commitment to Christ and His calling on our lives. In some areas, we have progressed from "empty" to "full," or at least up a notch or two. Let's brainstorm together some criteria we could use to evaluate our commitment to Christ.** Record their suggestions on the blank poster board. Some responses might include:

- *Time spent in God's Word*
- *Obedience to God's Word*
- *Prayer*
- *Fellowship*
- *Service*
- *Stewardship of resources, lifestyle*
- *Willingness to be a risk-taker*
- *Willingness to use my influence or position to further God's work*

Distribute more paper for each member. Instruct members to list some of the criteria mentioned and do a self-assessment, drawing a sample fuel gauge next to each criteria, with a needle pointing to whether they are more full or empty.

Ask them to discuss in pairs: **Where do I need the most work to become more committed? What would I like to make as my top three goals for increasing my commitment to Christ in the weeks ahead.**

Close with a few minutes of conversational prayer, thanking God for new insights and motivation gained during this study. Urge them to pray for increasing levels of commitment to knowing Christ and making Him known.